Dreams &

Dream Interpretation For Beginners

- Uncover The Hidden Meanings of

Your Dreams & 30 Amazing

Things You Can Do With Dowsing

Written By

Mia Rose

Content

Dreams

The Ultimate Dream Interpretation Guide

Uncover the Hidden Meanings of your Dreams

Written By

Mia Rose

Introduction

I want to thank you and congratulate you for getting the book, *"Dream Interpretation for Beginners – Uncover the Hidden Meanings of Your Dreams"*.

This book contains proven steps and strategies on how to interpret the meanings of your dreams.

Using traditional dream meanings passed down through the centuries, this book will teach you the basics of dream interpretation. The book looks at how the meaning of dreams has been a subject that has fascinated all human cultures, including our own. It examines why we place such importance on our dreams and what they may be able to reveal to us. The book explores which dreams may have important meanings and those that don't. It also looks at the key meanings that occur in many dreams relating to love, money and career. Along with the traditional meanings described here, the book also looks at how those meanings can be interpreted in the 21st century.

Thanks again for reading this book, I hope you enjoy it!

Chapter 1: Dreams; A Very Human Mystery

The meanings and understanding the meanings of dreams has been a preoccupation of humanity since, as far at it is possible to tell, we really first became human. While some supernatural or "occult" areas of study have been firmly dismissed by modern science, the study of dreams is one area in which science, or more specifically psychoanalysis, has continued to show much interest.

The human brain and the mind retain a level of mystery, even for scientists, and while techniques such as MRI scanning have allowed for a greater understanding of the physical makeup of the brain the true nature of the mind still remains, to a large extent, still shrouded in mystery. Psychoanalysis itself is a young science with beginnings only in the last hundred or so years. Humans, and their dreams, have however been around for much longer.

Today, many psychologists believe that dreams play a significant role in the workings of our mind and in contributing to our mental and emotional health. They seem, as far as can be established to help our brain to process the day's events, perhaps help us to work out difficult problems (both emotionally and practically) and appear to have a function for transferring knowledge and information into our unconscious or subconscious mind.

The latter function makes sense; our short term memory can only store so much information but much of what we learn in life needs to be stored "somewhere". It seems that our brains use a number of process to place important information, possibly everything we experience into the archive that is our unconscious mind. It's also understood by many psychoanalysts that this information affects our behavior even when we don't "remember" consciously the information stored in our brain.

Throughout our lives, as we store more information, our brain begins to build and notice patterns in life and in events around us. This may explain the way in which we instinctively understand what will happen next in many situations; our brains appear to forewarn us with complex and sometimes confusing dreams of coming events. In this context there is little that is occult or otherworldly about interpreting dreams and it can be seen as an expression of the sheer power of the human mind.

However modern science and psychology view dreams, historically, they have been viewed as significant. In the past they have often been variously seen as signs and omens. In many cultures they were (and are) viewed as direct messages from the dead, or from divine beings. People who experienced vivid dreams were considered especially blessed and, in many civilizations, those who could "interpret" dreams were seen as holy or revered individuals.

Interestingly, in both ancient traditions and modern science, although the theories differ, nearly every culture in both the past and present has given significance to dream meanings. They may expose our inner selves, our fears and desires or they may give us valuable information and insights which seem almost to have an occult source. Either way, few people do not attach meaning in some sense to our dreams.

So how much, or which version of our understanding of dreams is true? Perhaps none or perhaps something of many different theories has truth in it. Dreams are not unique to humans and many animals also appear to regularly dream. Dreams certainly seem to have some function and as science is only just beginning to truly explore the incredible power of that marvelous organ the "brain" perhaps, in time, a better understanding of how dreams function and what they truly are will become apparent.

One thing is, however, clear; dreams are extremely visual in their nature. They can be short snippets of images or feel like feature-length movies. They are rarely in print form and often not only (or purely) verbal. Dreams are about images and there may well be a good reason for this. Humans are intrinsically visual and sight has been one of the most important senses to us for much of our evolution. Our brains are wired to receive visual information far better than any other type of information.

Every other form of communication, more or less, we need to learn but (for most people) we don't need to learn to see. Nor do we need to really learn the meaning of some very basic symbols. We see simple things like safety and danger in color (red for danger, blue/green for safety). These symbols are almost universal. The human mind needs visual signals and stimuli to remember, interpret and understand. This may explain why our dreams are so very visual and often, very symbolic. They employ archetypes to get the message across to us – even if we don't want to hear that message!

Can Dreams Tell the Future?

Yes, no, maybe; dreams do, at times, seem to be able to do this. Some people may have more vivid and apparently psychic dreams than others. However, in some sense, dreams can be said to make, or influence, the future. A very strong dream, just before you wake, will leave a strong impression on your mind. It may seem strange, unlikely and the events may seem random (that, unfortunately is how dreams work!). However, in the following day, or days, events may unfold that bring the dream back to us. It will almost certainly (and however resistant to the dream you are) work on some level to govern your responses to those dreams. Whether this is an example of psychic ability or, more likely, an example of our brains working in a powerful way to bring about the results that we desire, we have yet to fully establish.

Whatever your view, dreams have for much of human history been used to understand ourselves better and to help us to see or foresee what is coming in life. This book takes a look at the common symbols found in dreams and the meanings that have been attributed to them over many hundreds of years.

Dream Interpretation; The Rules

The first rule of dream interpretation is to trust yourself! The second is to think before you interpret! The definitions in this book are taken from a wide variety of sources and many of them have been passed down from different sources, books or traditions over many centuries. Our dreams are very personal to us and the symbols that appear may mean something deeply personal to us, or may represent cultural archetypes. Interpreting dreams can take a little time and thought – what do the symbols and events in the dream relate to in your own life? When using the meanings in this book, try to place them in context within your own life.

As an example, imagine a dream in which you see a blacksmith smash your smart-phone to pieces! Centuries ago a blacksmith would be a common sight and a smart-phone would have been witchcraft (some might still view them that way!). Today, the opposites (more or less) apply!

You could look at the "meanings" for these symbols in this book or choose to interpret the meanings in relation to yourself. In centuries past a blacksmith was considered magical – perhaps a folk memory from very ancient times where these mysterious people turned stone into iron. That cultural mystery and sense of "otherness" remains and has found its way into more than one movie. However, real blacksmiths are rare creatures today and if you dream about one think about the wider meaning described in this book. In this dream the meaning could be that magical, external forces, creative forces, or even authority figures, are interfering with your ability to communicate! However, always interpret in the context of your own life; if you *are* a blacksmith, or know one, be more careful where you put your phone in future!

In short, always look at what the symbols in your dream mean to you. The meanings in this book relate to archetypal images and their most likely cultural meaning for many of us.

Dreams that Matter and Those that Don't

Traditional dream interpreters ascribe different levels of importance to different types of dream. They define three main categories and these are;

- Physical dreams; these are inspired by your physical health. If you are ill, your dreams may become confused or even delirious. In this category other physical stimuli can be included such as eating too much before bedtime! Usually these dreams occur early in the night and can be largely ignored.

- Dreams of memory; these are simply memories from the past that you relive in your dreams and they can be fairly obvious to identify. They may have no significance or they may represent issues that you need to deal with. Consider the dream, the impact it has on you, and the issues it's exploring.

- Dreams of significance; dreams *after* midnight are said to have more significance than those before. In our early stages of sleep we are "processing" the day. Later in the night our brain is organizing and analyzing information. This seems to be the time when it recognizes patterns and is when what appear to be "predictive" dreams may occur. Our brains are putting into place all the information we have stored up and they may, at this time, find answers to problems or foresee the likely outcome of current events most clearly. Traditionally, the later a dream occurs, especially if it occurs close to waking or after our normal waking time, it is the most important dream to heed.

Some sources suggest that dreams are governed by the law of contraries; for example, dreaming of a birth means a coming death or winning the lottery means losing money. However, most ancient sources agree that this is not the case; dreams tend to mean what they say. Working out *what* that is, is the hard part!

Recurring Dreams

These often are taken to have significant meaning and, perhaps, this is a fair point. They can be good or bad but usually indicate that our brain has something it wishes us to resolve. In many traditions a dream which comes three times in a short space of time is considered to be the most significant type of recurrent dream. These dreams are also, according to both tradition and anecdote, most likely to be warning dreams. Whatever the dream, the simple rule is to take heed if it repeats several times in a short space of time.

How to Use This Book

There are certain things in life that are universal to us as humans for survival. Our ancient brains often focus on these elements in life. The signs and symbols that our brains use seem on many occasions to fall into certain categories; food for our survival, shelter from the elements or danger and relationships. Food and shelter are our basic needs, while avoiding danger and finding safety in numbers have been human survival strategies since before we were fully human. Dreams that relate to these elements of our lives are significant, perhaps the most significant. In this book we use these basic categories and explore the most common meanings found throughout history, relating to them.

Chapter 2: Dream Meanings; Food and Sustenance

Sustenance is important to us all and dreams sometimes use obscure symbols to get their meaning across when relating to this subject. A dream about eating a delicious meal with a loved one may relate more to the meaning that we have a fulfilling relationship than to what is on the plate. Lack of food, or someone taking food from your plate, may not be about having a bad experience at a restaurant but simply suggest that the relationship with the person in their dream is not giving you what you need! Always be aware that dreams will use symbolic people. Eating with a parent (alive or dead) may symbolize authority or it may symbolize support and protection from the parent in question – or that you still have such support in life. In this section we'll look at some common, accepted meanings related to consuming food and drink.

Alcohol, Drunkenness

Though this may be related to real life events, beer, brewing or distilling were symbolic of many different things in many cultures. In many, brewed or distilled drinks were safer than water to drink and this cultural element may linger in some people's folk memory. Generally, brewing is a sign of success, but after delay. Drunkenness is variously interpreted as loss through foolishness or confusion and delays brought about by your own actions. Much depends on the context of this dream but it is generally a warning.

Banquets and Feasts

Food, in a party context in general, is to found in this category of dreams. If the celebrations go well and the food is plentiful this is a sign of success, often in work and business as well as in context of good friendships. If you see others eating but are not doing so yourself this is a sign of success to come but after a delay. Lack of food and/or a bad atmosphere indicates coming disappointment and possible failure. Generally, plenty in any sense in life is indicated by feast where large quantities of good food are available but the opposite is indicated where food is scarce or poor quality.

Bottles and Drinking Vessels

Generally, this is a sign of plenty and good fortune. If the liquid in the container is clear, pleasant and palatable, this means general good luck and indicates you have resources which will bring you strength. Broken drinking vessels indicate loss and poverty and may indicated broken or lost promises. This can relate to personal relationships, your own security or to work situations.

Butter

Commonly considered a positive omen, your efforts have been rewarded and completion, success and fulfillment are indicated by this dream. Modern day alternatives are included here! Any food which smells bad, is distasteful or dangerous indicates a negative outcome and in this case it suggests you fear that your efforts have been wasted.

Cakes and Confectionery

Considered, almost universally, a positive omen, especially for the young and for those embarking on new relationships. Plenty, comfort and happiness are all symbolized by cakes and confectionery.

Cheeses

Considered negative in dreams by many older sources, suggesting disappointment or loss. Some believe this may indicate a need to make detailed plans and be prepared for a long wait to see the results of your effort.

Cereal Crops

A very ancient and significant symbol, corn-fields, wheat-fields or other fields growing crops of any kind, are considered to be very significant dreams. They symbolize, when healthy, plenty, riches, wealth, good investments and even status. The stage of growth indicates where you may be in this cycle. Failed crops and diseased plants suggest the opposite but may act as a warning to look at your plans.

Crops, today, can include houseplants, or parks and gardens, as fewer of us are involved directly with agriculture!

Eggs

Once a staple food and a valuable replaceable source of protein. Eggs also symbolize birth, beginnings and potential in our minds. Eating eggs suggests you have created solid foundations for growth, buying or selling them suggests profit and good fortune. Broken eggs foretells bad decisions and loss. Much, in this case, will depend on the specifics of the dream and other symbols within it.

Fruit and Nuts

These are symbolic of good fortune, plenty and rest and relaxation in life. Like all foods the meaning can depend on the quality and quantity of the food. Bad, or lacking foods, mean lack of positive feelings in the area they relate to.

Meals

Different meanings have often been ascribed to different meals throughout the day. Breakfasts, especially plentiful ones, suggest energy and, in particular, mental energy; they indicate beginnings and the stamina to take initiative with these. Lunch suggests plenty in many traditional sources (breakfast and an evening meal were more common for most people in history). Evening meals suggest positive conclusions and an successful completion of projects. Again, much depends on the quality and quantity of the food and the company you keep in these dreams when interpreting them. Dreams about mealtimes are negative if food is bad, limited or arguments break out.

Milk

As with eggs this was, and is, an important commodity in many cultures. Meanings are very similar for both eggs and milk, success if you are drinking milk is usually indicated. Material gain and good fortune are generally associated with milk. Where the milk is bad, many sources suggest bad fortune. Some suggest that this may indicate you should look to use the resources you have in new, innovative ways.

Ovens

Including just about all manner of cooking implements. Generally this type of dream is considered fortunate. A hot oven with food cooking suggests plenty, good fortune, comfort and stability. It also suggests projects brought to fruition. Cold ovens, or empty pans suggest lack of resources in some area of life but are most often considered to suggest opportunity, new starts and that chances are coming that will allow you to create success. Negative aspects of this symbol include broken ovens or other cooking equipment, or ones that will not cook, despite apparently working. This suggests projects (or relationships) which you are trying to manage in the wrong way, with the wrong tools.

Chapter 3: Dream Meanings; Jobs and Money

Jobs and money, to most of us in the modern world, are primarily linked to our security and this in turn relates to the very basic human need for shelter. Whether you have a job to pay the bills or a career that you love, either way the issue of your security and ultimately shelter are strongly implicated in this area. In this section we'll take a look at some of the most significant dream interpretations relating to this need.

Ball Games

Many dream interpretations connect games, and ball games in particular, with financial affairs and employment. If you dream of having a ball thrown to you and catching it, this suggests coming opportunity and success. Be prepared! If you fail to catch the ball, or it rolls away from you, the meaning is generally interpreted as still being fortunate but you will face delays and missed opportunities before success is achieved.

Banks or Banking Transactions

If another person receives money through a bank or through a banking transaction in your dream this is a sign of disappointment, delay and failure in your endeavors. It may suggest that you are not being recognized, in some area of life but usually a work related area, for your efforts. Work here can mean employment, business or charity. To receive money in a dream is generally considered a good omen. It suggests promotion, new projects which will be successful and recognition for your hard work.

Beacons

A beacon, or any bright, shining, directional light, including lighthouses and or the headlights on vehicles is a dream of good fortune and prosperity. It often suggests safety, security and the end and completion of projects in a successful way. Bright lights generally signify safety and security but also an indication that you will receive help from others to bring about that result. It's also considered a strong indication of passing troubles and hope for the future. The dream may indicate that although prospects seem bleak, inspiration is at hand to turn a situation around.

Bees

Symbolically bees are signs of hard work and achievement. Success is nearly always indicated if you dream of bees; in most cases this will be through sheer determination, attention to detail and hard work. A small number of bees indicate these are the qualities you must learn to apply now while a larger number suggests your efforts are close to reward and you have the skills you need already. To be stung by a bee or bees indicates almost exactly what it suggests, the hard won success may come at a cost in other areas of life and may be barbed with regret.

Counting

Linked to success and accumulation, but if you make mistakes during the process this suggests a delay before both are achieved. A warning to be scrupulous and pay attention to details is often suggested in this case. Business projects will soon show positive results if the counting is easy and accurate. If it is slow and labored, much work will be required to achieve your goals.

Communications

Letters, emails, texts, phones, the Internet and social networks can all be included in this category! Dreams about communication were, at one time much simpler – usually referring to letters or telegrams. However, the basic rules apply in whatever form you dream about communication! To see somebody else reading a letter meant for you (reading your texts, hacking your Facebook account!) warns of betrayal in some form or other. This usually indicates the breaking of promises or secrets being exposed. Dreams connected to communication generally relate to emotions and relationships but can also relate to business. In this context, seeing another read your "letter" may suggest you are giving too much away, or have rivals seeking to better you by deceit. Receiving a "letter" in most contexts means news of coming change – this can be positive or negative and may depend on the context in the dream.

Fabric

Any kind of fabric is often related to business and work related ventures. Good quality, beautiful or intricate fabrics indicate positive outcomes, success and abundance. Poor quality suggests there is some flaw in your endeavor. New fabrics suggest opportunities will come to you soon and you would be wise to take them. Old fabric suggest that whatever you are working on has had its day – it's time to move on.

Royalty

For the modern world we should include political leaders here as well. This is generally considered to be both a sign of great fortune close at hand and general prosperity. It's also considered to suggest a rise in status (promotion is a strong possibility). This dream warns of coming opportunity and it usually does refer to the world of work and business; the opportunity may seem too good to be true when it comes but this dream advises you to take it.

Towers

Including towering buildings of all kind. Symbols of strength, power and defense, dreams in which you enter and climb a tower suggest projects that will come to success. Much will depend on the nature of the dream and your relation to the building. If you encounter difficulties in climbing the building this suggests success is possible but you must take care in your approach. Broken, or falling towers, are signs of sudden change of fortune (usually but not always) in a negative way. Towers under construction (especially if you're involved) denote hard work but great achievement is promised.

Treasure

Digging for treasure (or winning the lottery) is a complicated dream – and a very old one. It has a number of meanings and much depends on the context. It can mean fruitless labor – and in a business sense this can mean you should consider your next move or the usefulness of your current role/project. If you find treasure this usually indicates that your labors will be rewarded in the end – but the search or the effort could be long. Generally considered a warning that there are easier ways to achieve the goal for which you are aiming.

Volcanoes and Earthquakes

Another strange dream which can relate to any area of life. In terms of work and business this is a sign, not surprisingly, of sudden change. Dormant volcanoes indicate danger and trouble ahead, which may overtake you suddenly (redundancies, closures, lost orders or legal problems).

Active volcanoes and earthquakes suggest that the time for action (probably change) is now. The dream usually relates to events which are beyond our control. This dream is a warning, in most cases, to be prepared! The dream itself is not necessarily a bad dream but indicates that you sense something is "wrong" with a situation. The outcome can depend on your response in the real world.

Chapter 4: Dream Meanings; Love and Relationships

Humans are social animals, perhaps the *most* social, and our survival has long depended on our ability to build relationships with other people. Whether that's in the context of work, play or at home our relationships with others define us. Most of us are deeply intuitive (whether we realize it or not) when it comes to our personal relationships in every area of our life. We know when something is "wrong", when something is "right". This is instinctive and it comes from years (tens of thousands of them) of experience. Our intuitive knowledge is often buried deep inside our unconscious minds – how often have you felt uncomfortable around a new acquaintance or associate for no "reason"? On most occasions your first instinct will have proved right. In our dreams, signs and symbols will frequently appear that will "tell" us things we need to know about our relationships. They can be both positive and negative and usually it's wise to take note of them. In this chapter we'll look at some of the ways in which our brain most commonly tries to get these messages across.

Altar

Generally, to dream of a wedding is a sign of disappointment. Contrary though this may seem, most sources agree on this.

This can be interpreted as misplaced trust or of promises that may not be kept. In other contexts an altar symbolizes judgment in some form and indicates that you should search your heart for your true feelings – generally in relation to an emotional situation.

Beauty

In any form, this is a sign of love and happiness. If you are beautiful yourself in the dream it suggests a happy love life and one with great potential. To see beautiful people in your dream is a sign that you are loved very deeply. It is also considered to be a sign of great success in area of life but is particularly related to relationships – be they with partners or friends.

Candles

A very, very old symbol which we can substitute for "light sources" in all their modern variety. A bright candle, or light, tells us that we have a trustworthy friend or companion who is watching over us. A low, faltering light (guttering candle in older sources) suggests that gossip and rumor is being spread about you. Friends may not be what they seem in this case.

Crowds

Generally, a good dream which foretells good times around the corner, parties, holidays, friends and happy friendships.

The nature and mood of the crowd should be taken into account but generally this dream suggests good times, social events and happiness. This can even be true if the crowd seems hostile; in this instance you may be feeling nervous about an event but the dream suggests that your fears are unfounded.

Father (or Father-figure)

Whether your real father is alive or dead, dreaming of an individual who fulfills this role for you is considered to be a very significant dream indeed. If the father offers advice it should be heeded, if he seems happy or sad try to understand the source of this emotion. Whatever this figure expresses take note as it's likely to be an important message that your brain is trying to get across to you. Dreams of this nature can be very personal to the individual and deserve attention and thought as to their true meaning.

Jewelry

To dream of wearing jewelry indicates that you have an admirer who has yet to make them-self known to you. This is considered a fortunate dream in many respects and the brighter or newer the jewelry appears the more likely that you will discover who your admirer is in the near future. Tarnished, dirty or damaged jewelry is still believed to denote an admirer but the individual may be less than trustworthy. This dream may be a warning.

Mother (or Mother Figure)

Much the same as father, this dream is also seen as a promise of help and loving friends. If you are facing problems or worries you will find help readily given. This may come from your real mother or it may come through close friends or relatives. This dream suggests that you should confide your worries in someone you trust and help and solutions will be found. As with a father-figure dream this can be a very personal dream but nearly always suggest selfless support is available should you choose to seek it.

Moonlight and the Moon

Dreaming of the moon is considered to be a sign of great good fortune for those in love. If the moonlight is clouded it is still considered a good sign; though troubles may loom in the future, they will pass. In general this is a sign of great good fortune in love and of happy outcomes in romantic relationships.

Music

To dream of music is believed to suggest that you will hear from old friends or reconnect with people who are important to you. Its a sign of friendship but especially of the renewal of friendship. If the music is sad this can be a sign of problems with a friend and the possible loss of that friendship. It's often a dream of significance, whichever the case, and should be acted upon quickly.

Religious Figures

To dream of any religious figure is, in many traditions, taken to be a sign of coming disappointment in a relationship. Be careful of the context here; if you are planning to be married the dream is less likely to have any significance other than you will, in many cases, have to deal with a figure of this sort. If you aren't planning (or already are married) the warning of disappointment is likely to be more significant.

Water

Water is an element strongly associated with emotions; water in this sense can mean ponds, pools, baths, rivers, streams or whole oceans. To dream of clear calm water suggests all is well in your relationships. To dream of dark, stormy or muddy water suggests trouble in your personal life. Traveling over stormy water indicates the most difficult problems. Unclear water suggests that there are secrets or hidden elements to the trouble. The outcome of the dream is often important, stormy waters becoming calm means a positive outcome is on its way while the opposite means there is trouble brewing.

Chapter 5: General Dream Symbolism

Dreams are all about symbols; as stated earlier in the book we are very visual creatures. This is our intrinsic and default nature; we can communicate with anybody from anywhere by using symbols, images and signs. In the twentieth century, when man first began to explore beyond the planet on which we live, spacecraft set to travel beyond our own solar system were sent off containing images on the basis that intelligent life elsewhere in the universe would understand symbols rather than be easily able to decipher our languages.

In this final chapter we'll explore common symbols in the context of our dreams. These images may have very specific meanings in your own life but many are universal to all of us. One area where some "messages" from the brain may not be universal is the symbolism behind colors. The meaning and association of some colors is different in different cultures; in many western cultures, for example, red is associated with danger, but in China and other eastern cultures the color is associated with good luck and prosperity. This book focuses on dream interpretations in the western tradition – if you're cultural background is none-western, consider the implications of colors in your own culture when interpreting your dreams.

Colors In Dreams

In this section we'll look only at the black, white and the primary colors red, blue and green. Other colors are a combination of these and the influences of each color will be "colored" according to their predominance. Many people don't dream in color and when colors dominate a dream it is often an important sign, which suggests the dream is of strong significance.

- Black; traditionally associated with bad news, loss or grief, black can also mean change and secrecy. Major changes in life (hence the association with death) are often signified if a dream is "colored" by this tone. Death itself is not necessarily indicated but can be interpreted as the death of ideas, or a relationship. Generally, the color warns that big changes are either coming or are needed in your life.

- White; as with black this is a color that has been associated with mourning (in both western and eastern cultures). In traditional interpretations the color is seen to indicate change, in much the same way as black. It is also seen to indicate a "blank canvas" and represent opportunities to begin a new chapter in life. The color also symbolizes purity, newness, beginnings and honesty. However, some sources state that where white dominates a dream it can indicate a "white-wash" - that things are being covered up or that secrets are being kept. Interpreting this kind of dream can be complex and white has associations with spirituality; it can suggest the hidden, the unknown and new opportunity all at the same time. Often the best advice to take from this dream is that you have the opportunity to begin afresh but should take care to establish facts.

- Black and White; generally this is taken to suggest that you are seeing things in real life in black and white! This can be a warning that you need to view a situation with more objectivity and awareness that there are possibly many different perspectives on an issue or situation. Consider the message of the dream carefully and look for alternative views or advice on the matter that the dream seems to be related to.

- Blue; this color suggest wisdom, honesty, intellect, peace and creativity. This is the color of clarity of thought and can suggest that you need to bring your intellectual capabilities to the matter at the heart of the dream. Blue has another side to it – the color of the oceans and water it relates to deep emotional contacts and bonds in a positive way. Blue indicates that you have good friends or loved ones in your life and indicates peace and happiness in matters of the heart.

It indicates honesty and trust in personal relationships.

- Red; traditionally this is interpreted as a warning in dreams. Red indicates danger, anger, destructive tendencies and sudden change. It has associations with fire – which can be both destructive and renewing. Some sources ascribe passion and energy to red as a color and it can certainly indicate this in dreams. Many dreams featuring this color call for swift, decisive and clear action over the matter in hand. Darker reds suggest anger, particularly suppressed anger, while lighter tones, those towards oranges and pink foretell the potential for powerful, rapid changes. Very vibrant reds can warn that you may need to stop and think about your actions before taking them.

- Green; the associations of green for most of humanity are positive. The color indicates fertility, growth, prosperity and abundance. This can be in any or all areas of life. It can signify a coming birth, a change (for the better) in circumstances. Darker greens suggest things coming to fruition, to completion and the reaping of rewards after labor. Lighter greens suggest the beginnings of new projects that will be successful. Growth, fulfillment and personal achievement are all signified by this color and it many cultures it is strongly associated with good luck. Darker shades of green have also long been associated with financial prosperity.

Death in Dreams

Death is a fundamental fear in humanity and it appears in dreams in many guises. However, it is not, traditionally, believed to interpret impending death either of the dreamer or the person dreamed of. To dream you see yourself dead, often indicates a sudden change of circumstances (this can be positive or negative) and a leap into the unknown. If you see another person dead this can indicate impending illness, or betrayal in a friendship or relationship – the individual may become "dead" to you. Generally, dreams in which death appears to feature are a warning of some kind that change is on its way or is urgently needed. To dream of death is not, however, a negative dream at all, it simply strongly suggests change and this change can often be for the good.

Landscapes

Landscapes appear in all of our dreams. They can be familiar places or places that we know that take on different, unrecognized forms. Sometimes we dream of specific landscape features; woodlands, mountains, open countryside and cityscapes. The meaning of the dream is often impacted by the nature of the landscape, if it feels threatening it is a warning, while a pleasant landscape indicates positive outcomes. The following symbolic landscapes often appear in dreams, although the meanings should be, again, interpreted in some context with your own life.

- Forests and Woodlands; forests were the wild-lands, filled with fear, danger and uncertainty for our ancestors. They were places to avoid, places of mystery and confusion. In a forest it is impossible to get a clear sight-line, and between the trees, it can be hard to make out what that movement from the corner of our eyes was. However, forests were also strongly associated with the "other" in this sense meaning other worlds, the spiritual and the divine. In our dreams forests and woodlands can have both of these meanings. Generally, if the forests or woodlands in our dreams are dark, tangled and intimidating places this suggests fear, anxiety and a sense of lack of control. They are strongly indicative that we feel lost, cut off from society, or alienated in some sense. Searching for a loved one in a forest indicates you feel cut-off from them, have lost a sense of connection or simply lost contact with them. Being hunted or chased in a forest can mean you have enemies in some area of your life; or that others are deceiving you, leading you down false paths or leading you astray.

Bright, sunny, lush forests have very much the opposite meanings to the former. Usually this type of dream features more open woodland. This dream has associations with peace, with a deep spirituality and connection to your inner self. If you feel confident in the setting this is a sign that you will prosper in life and that you will draw on your own inner strength, belief and creativity to achieve your ends. This is a very positive dream for artists, scientists and also for new parents! This is a dream that indicates independence and self-reliance and tells us that we have enough of both to make a great success of our lives.

- Mountains; a mountain or mountain range has a number of different meanings in dream interpretation. In many cultures mountains were, like forests, wild places and often were obstacles to travel. In dreams they can be placed in several contexts. If you are climbing a mountain this means that you must make great effort to achieve your goals, the road is likely to be long and dangerous. Much will depend on your own emotions and attitude in the dream. To struggle and give up means that you are unwilling to preserver in your task – and it may not be worth it. To continue on doggedly can indicate you have the strength and stamina you need. To reach the top of a mountain suggests success – great success – but this may depend on the view. If it's clear, wide and spectacular you will – after effort – achieve your dreams and goals in life. Obscured or cloudy views, in this case, mean that the efforts you are making will not bring positive results or that they will not be worth the effort you have invested. Dreams relating to mountains can relate to any area of life – relationships, finances or career. They indicate great obstacles which must be conquered and the outcome of the dream can offer you insight into whether or not you should pursue the course of action you are currently on.

- Open Countryside; again, common in dreams, but with very variable meanings. The underlying message in this dream is opportunity and particularly the opportunity for success. As with mountains, this can relate to any area of our life. Career and wealth are often associated with dreams of open landscapes but all areas of life can be indicated. Much will depend what is currently on your mind or the focus of your life. The appearance of the landscape and the conditions of both the weather and your own attitude are the key points to take note of if this type of dream occurs. If you feel threatened, exposed or afraid of the landscape this can indicate that you are holding yourself back in some way – that opportunity is there but you need the skills to take it and, importantly, the courage to do so. Where you feel confident and safe within the setting the dream indicates that you have the skills to make the most of the opportunities that come to you. This dream is extremely lucky and promises success in many areas of life. Where the landscape appears overgrown, neglected or the weather conditions make it threatening, this is a sign that much work is needed to bring your opportunities to fruition. It can also indicate that you are not making the most of your skills, talents and the opportunities that present themselves in life. Take this dream as a warning – you have everything you need for great success but are not using it to your best advantage. Open countryside of fields filled with ripening or ripened crops is also an excellent omen, success in this case is very close at hand.

- Cities and Cityscapes; cities are very new additions to the landscape in terms of both the planet's history and human history. They are indicative of order, civilization of wealth, opportunity and relaxation and ease in life. They are also highly symbolic of commerce and trade. While dreams in cityscapes often indicate business, work and wealth they can also relate to other areas of life. Today, most of us live in cities or urban environments and the meaning of dreams relating to them may also indicate our homes, security and safety. Generally, as with many dreams, our attitude and feelings towards the city in the dream indicate the meaning of the dream. Where we feel happy, comfortable, safe and familiar with a city, this suggests real opportunity and prosperity in matters relating to work, business, trade and new ventures. It is also suggestive of good friends, of socializing of opportunities to enjoy ourselves. Cities can be strongly representative of our civilized side. If you are happily exploring a strange city consider this a sign that new interests and valuable opportunities are coming your way. When negative, a cityscape will look dangerous, rundown or a feeling of being lost or fearful will dominate the dream. This indicates that we are concerned about our jobs, our careers or that we have deep rooted fears of interactions with others. We may have taken business decisions (or be about to) that we have misgivings about. We may lack much connection in our lives with culture or civilization and need to connect more with the outside world.

Conclusion

Thank you again for reading this book!

I hope this book has given you insight into your own sign of the Zodiac and that of your friends and family and also highlighted some areas which are overlooked in modern Astrology.

Finally, if you enjoyed this book, please take the time to share your thoughts and post a review on Amazon. It'd be greatly appreciated!

Thank you and good luck!

Dowsing

30 Amazing Things You Can Do With Dowsing

Written By

Mia Rose

Introduction

I want to thank you and congratulate you for getting the book, "Dowsing; 30 Amazing Things You Can Do With Dowsing".

This book contains proven steps and strategies on how to learn and practice the art of Dowsing. The history of dowsing is obscure but dowsing has been widely used since at least the 15th century to identify minerals, ore and water sources. Falling in and out of favor over the centuries it has been seen as useful engineering tool and/or a dark art linked to witchcraft! This reputation has fluctuated and dowsing became popular with companies searching for oil in the 19th and early 20th centuries but at the same time saw renewed interest from those fascinated by the paranormal world.

This book looks at the history, the practice and techniques of dowsing as they are currently understood. Dowsing is not a art that needs special skills but simply requires practice. This book will teach you all you need to know in order to learn the art. In addition, in the second part of the book, we've listed 30 fun, interesting and useful ways you can use Dowsing. Hopefully, this list will provide you with inspiration and many ideas for alternative uses for dowsing.

Thanks again for reading this book, I hope you enjoy it!

Part One

Dowsing, the History and Practice

Dowsing has been practiced for hundreds, possibly thousands, of years as a technique to find underground sources of water, minerals, gems, oil and even bodies. Today, the technique remains popular if often greeted with skepticism by science – although not quite as much skepticism as you might expect! The basic definition of dowsing is "searching or finding"; this can be applied in the traditional sense of finding water sources or minerals or in a wider sense, often used today, meaning to seek answers.

What Is Dowsing?

Traditional Dowsing uses rods of different kinds which the Dowser carries in their hands to locate the item that is being sought. Rods were usually formed from some kind of twig – the most common being hazel or willow rods. Modern techniques have adapted the concept and metal rods are now a common tool that many dowsers use. The actual material that the rod is formed from appears to have no effect on the working of the rod; as the dowser paces the area being checked the rods respond by crossing or by pointing downwards when the item being sought is passed over.

Modern dowsing also includes the use of pendulum dowsing, which simply involves a heavier item held from a piece of cord or string. This method is usually used in contexts where the dowser does not need to move around and the pendulum acts as pointer, usually towards letters, lines, symbols or numbers written down on paper or card.

The History of Dowsing

Records as to how and when dowsing came from are few and far between but it appears to have been commonly used in 15th century central Europe (particularly Germany) mainly as a means to locate metals. It is, however, unlikely that the technique sprang from nowhere to address this requirement but instead was developed from a far older technique for sourcing underground water.

The term "dowsing" seems to have originated in England sometime in the 16th century, where the expanding mining industries in many parts of the country used German miners and techniques to both construct mines and also to find the best locations for them in the first place. This was the first heyday of dowsing for mineral deposits and the practice became widespread.

Dowsing came under considerable negative scrutiny in this period from the Church and it is probably at this point that the technique became identified as an "occult" method of discovering hidden information or even wealth. From being a purely practical engineering solution to being seen as a possible magical (and therefore dangerous) skill, dowsing became increasingly less popular with mainstream science and gradually gathered a reputation for being a superstitious practice that should, at best, be frowned upon.

Dowsing, as a folk skill, however, continued to be practiced quietly in many rural communities. In this context the primary information sought was the location of underground water supplies. This, as mentioned above, was probably the earliest use for dowsing and although it fell out of fashion in the mining industry it remained a highly valued skill in many small communities – although not one that sought to advertise itself too widely given the attitude of both the church and wider society!

By the late 19th and early 20th centuries the hunt for oil was on and, as with the explosion in mining in the 15th century, competition to find lucrative drilling sites led to the return of dowsing to the mining, drilling and engineering field. Dowsing had continued to be quietly practiced in many rural communities in Europe and had been "exported" as a traditional skill to the Americas. Here it had proved helpful in other, new, small rural communities in the search for reliable water supplies. The suddenly urgent need to discover suitable sites for oil drilling saw resurgence in interest in this traditional technique. Dowsers found themselves sought after individuals once more and their skills were used to help locate this new type of mine!

During the 20th century dowsing continued for find popularity within the oil industry, although often large companies were unwilling to publicly admit that they used this form of "witchcraft" to locate the most lucrative sites to drill! Dowser too, with centuries of traditional circumspection brought on by a certain amount of persecution were not always keen to admit that they were involved! By the late 20th century, despite scientific skepticism about the technique remaining strong, the use of dowsing in military settings was relatively common and the US Marines deployed the technique in the search for hidden weapons, tunnels and mines of a very different kind. Police forces too, in many parts of the world, employed the arts of the dowser to assist in finding missing persons or locate graves of the victims of crimes.

The Other 20th Century History

During the 20th century dowsing gathered a very different following from its traditional supporters in the mining and engineering industry! Esoteric groups and those fascinated by the paranormal all began to explore the "lost" art of dowsing.

One early pioneer was the British archaeologist Thomas Lethbridge; Lethbridge had a respected reputation as an Anglo-Saxon archaeologist but later in life became fascinated by the paranormal. Lethbridge conducted numerous experiments with a new way of dowsing using a pendulum and he even developed a scale which could be used to in the more practical elements of dowsing for minerals.

This led to new methods of dowsing being developed for new purposes. The basic understanding of dowsing remained the same – in that it is a technique for "finding". However, this new context involved users searching for different types of answer. The technique soon became identified with Spirit Guides, or ghosts and spirits in general. One extremely well known version of "dowsing" is the Ouija Board; where a pendulum or pointer is used to identify letters in order to communicate with the dead.

As the New Age revolution spread in the 1960s the power of dowsing to answer questions relating to health, spiritual development and even past life knowledge were all rapidly developed and the technique could, to some extent, be said to have come full circle once more, being now more associated with the spiritual, the occult and with magic, than simply being a great way to find a new well or make a fortune from oil!

Who Uses Dowsing Today?

Supporters of dowsing as a technique for finding water or mineral deposits are found in some surprising places. In many small rural communities dowsing remains an accepted practice with some locals being known as being natural dowsers. Generally these practitioners are called upon to find water supplies, or buried cables or old drains. In these communities – often hard working and hard headed in many ways – dowsing is not seen as anything out of the ordinary but simply as a practical tool to be used when needed. At the other end of the spectrum, surprising users can also be found, including the Soviet government in the not-so-recent past who happily used those with dowsing abilities to search for mineral or oil deposits. Some governments still sanction the use of dowsers in Europe and the use of professional dowsers has never entirely fallen out of fashion. Occasionally, in the mainstream press, articles appear about the use of dowsing in cases of lost people, or by major companies searching for mineral or oil deposits. While dowsing may have a reputation as an "occult" or esoteric, it seems that it remains in use in many surprising, if under-reported, settings!

How Does Dowsing Work?

This question has been asked since at least those early days when European mining speculators searched for mineral deposits and, despite some study, the answer is as yet unclear. Some people claim that dowsing doesn't work, or can't work. There are, however, many others including both experienced dowsers and surprised novice dowsers who simply state that it does!

There is no simple answer to the question of if, how or why dowsing works and the answers that you will find range from the bizarre to the unlikely and back again! Many spiritualists argue that it is the world of spirit that explains dowsing while many supporters suggest that the human body reacts to magnetic fields and resonances given off by certain substances or minerals. This reaction creates small and normally imperceptible movements within the muscles, causing them to influence the movement of the rods used in dowsing. Dowsing is, however, controversial and how it works is explained by many different groups, in different ways. Some of these groups and their views are described below;

What the New Age Lobby Says;

Generally, it depends on the tradition you approach for an answer on this one! To a Wiccan it will be the universal force of the God and Goddess to which they attribute the power of dowsing. To a Spiritualist you'll undoubtedly find that the world of spirit is usually considered responsible. To those interested in Eastern religions, the forces of universal energy will be the most likely source of the power behind dowsing. However, most traditions will readily accept that the technique not only works but can be used in many beneficial ways.

What Science Says;

In general, science says that there is no established proof that dowsing works. Studies and tests have, so far, returned only results that suggest there is no greater success when dowsing than would be the case for pure chance. However, science does establish that some species of animal, fish and birds have very clear responses to magnetic fields although human responses to those same fields is not clearly understood. Scientific study so far does not link this to possible or probably links to human dowsing capabilities.

What the Dowsers Say;

"It works". This is the most likely response that you'll get from amateur and professional dowsers. Interestingly, even amongst normally straightforward people in those traditional, rural communities you'll get the same answer from dowsers. In even the most unlikely individuals in these communities you'll also find that the skill remains relatively common and that many people don't worry too much about the reason it works but simply accept it as a useful tool.

Using Dowsing for Personal Gain

You'll find that many sources of information on dowsing strongly advise against using dowsing for personal gain or for "negative purposes". However, this is somewhat at odds with the traditional (or even modern day commercial uses of the technique). Those early mining speculators for gold, iron ore and tin were not dowsing for minerals simply out of the good of their hearts, or to benefit society as a whole. They were using the technique for the more prosaic, if less spiritually enlightened, ends of (their own) wealth creation! Even water dowsing was for personal benefit and traditional dowsers who use their skills to find water and/or oil today rarely do so without a fee structure firmly in mind.

Ultimately it is down to you to consider your own beliefs and ethics when dowsing for anything. Dowsing may be nothing more than an innate human skill which we simply don't understand as well as other human skills. Or it may be an expression of some greater force than us – a universal energy or being of some kind. Either way, living a life that is ethical and in which we strive not harm others by our actions is never a bad plan! There is almost certainly no reason or obstacle to using dowsing to achieve ends which benefit you; how you approach that or whether you do is entirely up to you!

Learning to Dowse

There are numerous techniques and tips available in order to dowse. Some may require a little more effort and persistence than others. The real key to the skill actually seems to be practice. In this section we'll take a brief look at the main ways in which you can begin to learn to employ this amazing, if sometimes unnerving, technique.

The Traditional Method

This is the most basic way of dowsing and as can be expected from its practitioners, those hard-headed, practical countrymen and women, there's nothing too complicated about it. You'll need a couple of rods, your hands and something to search for.

1. The rods can be anything you have readily to hand; the most traditional type are made from twigs of hazel or willow – which traditional country dowsers would have found to be the most readily found items to hand! Today, even traditional dowsers will use metal rods. A popular option is old clothes hangers, cut up into an L-shape, which can be held loosely in the hand with the longer part of the L extending in front of the dowser. Some people have happily used paper clips, twisted to shape.

2. Hold, but don't grip, the rods so that they extend in front of you, roughly parallel to each other. Pace an area where you are likely to find the object, material or mineral of choice.

3. You can use this technique indoors and search for electrical cables or plumbing pipes in your home. However, it's more fun to search for an object hidden by a friend, and better still to do so outdoors!

4. Stand slightly open mouthed and disbelieving with shock when the rods react! They will and it can be an unnerving moment when this first occurs. The sensation can be relatively light or, for some, very strong and sudden but the rods will make a clear movement and often a determined pull.

Tips; often dowsing is a very personal thing; not everyone finds the rods react in the same way. For some they cross when the sought after item if found and for others they swing backwards away from each other. Both of these movements can either indicate you are getting closer or further away from the object you are seeking. Understanding the response is the first step and for this reason it makes sense to practice with an object that you know is definitely there and one which has been hidden by a friend! You can attempt this exercise as often as you like, for as long as you like. Gradually you'll find that your skill improves and you develop a better feeling for the response.

Pendulum Techniques

These techniques have been developed in more recent years although it's possible they have been used in the past to search for answers, people and other information. You'll need a "pendulum", your hands, a relevant chart, a spare pen and paper along with something to seek for. In this case the latter can be "knowledge" of some kind or, again, a physical, hidden object. Before we take you through a simple Pendulum technique exercise we'll look at the (slightly more complex) equipment you need.

- Pendulums; these are, very simply, heavy objects suspended from cord or string. You can purchase expensive, attractive and decorative pendulums for dowsing online or from Esoteric stores, or simply get a pebble and tie it to some string. The options in between are as endless as you care to think of and only limited by your imagination. The key properties of the pendulum include the length of string, which initially is best decided by your own height and your preferred position for dowsing (sitting or standing) and the weight of the object. This latter should be neither too heavy nor too light. A feather will be no use and a 50 pound weight will be equally useless. As mentioned, pebbles can be great but many small household objects will work well. Pendulums with certain lengths can be used to identify specific objects or materials, according to Tom Lethbridge's method and we'll look at those later in this section. However, to begin to learn the technique, a medium length pendulum of simple construction will be perfectly adequate.

- Charts; these help to make pendulum dowsing sound just that bit more esoteric and mystical than it really needs to! Charts, in this context, can be as simple or as complicated as you like. Charts usually incorporate numbers or letters or both; if you're asking a question you'll need to be able to spell out the answer. For this reason a chart with all the letters of the alphabet is often used, or one with the numbers 0-9 (don't worry, this will be plenty of numbers). You can create your own handwritten one, although you should be able to find examples online. Ideally, create a chart in a semi-circle; for example with "A" or "0" placed to the left of the paper and "Z" or "9" to the right, directly opposite each other. The other symbols should be placed consecutively, rising to the mid-point and falling to the other side of the paper. This allows the pendulum to clearly swing in an easy to read direction.

- Yes or No? As with traditional dowsing, pendulums tend to respond to different people in different ways. "Yes" may be signified by an anti-clockwise circle, or a clockwise one. "No" will be the opposite direction. However, the pendulum may swing back and forth or side to side for you. Test these out by drawing circles and lines showing each direction and then a second set of circles and lines with the word "yes" or "no" noted within/next to them. Simply lightly grip the string or cord of the pendulum and hold it over each. You can encourage it to swing over the initial set of images but let it choose its own "Yes" or "No". This can take anything from several attempts to much practice. Be patient!

Pendulum Practice

1. Hold the pendulum in the hand that you don't normally write with; this makes it significantly easier to make a note of any replies to your question. Keep your grip light, but strong enough to hold the pendulum in place.

2. Begin your attempts by establishing what your "yes" and "no" pendulum responses are. This may take some time and you may need to take a break as you experience the apparently "magical" movements of the pendulum for the first time!

3. Once you're clear on the responses from the pendulum you can ask a question. Again, a hidden object in your home can be a good starting point. You can simply ask if the object is in specific

rooms, on the first floor or higher floors. Try to frame your questions in a way in which a simple "yes or no" answer will help you identify the location.

4. Generally it is easier to start you pendulum dowsing practice with simple questions. Once you have some experience you can use more complex questions which require the answer (literally) spelling out, as mentioned above.

Concentration or Zoning Out?

The oddest part of dowsing, perhaps the most magical, is the "how do the rods know what I'm looking for?" question. Dowsing is a technique that can help you find anything from buried treasure to a blocked drainage pipe. How this actually works is the biggest mystery and how you "tune" yourself to the desired object is still unclear. The simplest way is to focus and focus very hard on the object, mineral, person, substance or question you are searching for. The most likely explanation for the effectiveness of dowsing is probably connected to a strong role played by the subconscious mind, acting in conjunction with tiny micro-movements of the muscles. Use focus and a clear mind to concentrate on your purpose and your results will be most effective. Some people find that meditation techniques can help, while others seem to be able to focus very easily.

It may be important to note that many traditional practitioners (those mostly involved in water and mineral sourcing) don't focus too hard or concentrate on too much. They simply accept that the rods will respond when they cross what is being searched for. Practice, in many areas of life, will identify the way which works best for you.

Lethbridge Pendulum Lengths

As mentioned above, Tom Lethbridge, an early pioneer in the art of pendulum dowsing established a series of lengths of pendulum to use when searching for specific substances or qualities. These are detailed below and you may wish to adopt them for your dowsing practice;

Material	Length (inches)
Sulfur	7
Graphite	10
Carbon	12
Slate, concrete	13
Glass, porcelain	14
Quartzite, flint	15 ½

Organic matter including coal	20
Silver lead, salt	22
Vegetable oil, amber	23 ½
Masculinity, diamond	24
Alcohol	25 ½
Running water	26 ½
Femininity, gold	29
Copper, brass, tin	30 ½
Iron	32
Death, anger	40

Part Two

Amazing Things You Can Do With Dowsing

Hopefully, the first part of this book has helped you to understand what dowsing is, and how to begin practicing it. This second section is designed to give you some ideas for how you can use dowsing and what the most common ways are in which it has been used. We've gathered together many different uses from a wide range of traditions and sources. The aim in this part of the book is not to suggest that you do use dowsing for all or any of these ends, simply to give you an idea of what others have found dowsing to be useful or effective for. Some are simple, straightforward and have fairly obvious practical benefits. Others may only be relevant to individuals with certain beliefs or interests. I hope you enjoy this part of the book and it gives you a starting point for your own exploration of dowsing.

Practical Uses For Dowsing

Water Witching, Diving and Dowsing

Almost certainly the oldest and most practically useful reason to dowse for anything! This is where it all began for dowsing. You can dowse for water anywhere and it may be most useful if you need a new domestic/farm supply, or know somebody who does. It can also be useful for working out where blockages occur in drains, or pipes and cables are damaged. Simply use rods, pace the area in question and wait for a response.

Depth of Water to Drill For

Again, traditional dowsing at its best! Use a number chart, combined with questions such as "How many thousands/hundreds of feet is water located at?" You'll need to ask several times to get a specific answer; start with thousands, see where the pendulum indicates and then ask again in lower terms (hundreds, tens, and finally in single units).

Amount/Suitability of Water Available

You can use pendulum dowsing to find out if the amount of water is suitable for your proposed use; for example for crops or as a domestic supply. In addition, check if the supply is suitable or safe for use. If rod dowsing, simply keep the questions in mind as you identify different potential sources, see if you get a yes in some locations and no in others.

Drill Sites for Oil or Minerals

Again, this is one of the more traditional uses for dowsing. Generally, most people will be able to dowse in this way but only those with many years of practice will be the most effective. Some individuals will have strong natural dowsing abilities and moving into the potentially lucrative career of dowsing for these substances may be an attractive option.

Buried Treasure

It may, or may not, be a coincidence that Tom Lethbridge was an archaeologist. If you're interested in history (or large hoards of buried treasure) dowsing for either is a use you'll find attractive. You can use pendulum dowsing combined with a map to identify likely sites and rod dowsing to locate specific fascinating artifacts (or large hoards of buried treasure) in much the same way as others use metal detectors!

Electrical Cables

Dowsing for buried cables is one of the more prosaic and highly practical uses for dowsing; great on building sites or when re-developing your home. It's usually best accomplished with rod dowsing and a plan to identify likely cables. Only consider any excavation with relevant safety advice or appropriate contractors, depending on circumstances.

Plumbing Problems

Whether you're searching for blocked drains or plumbing pipes in your home, dowsing can be a highly effective technique for locating them. This is a similar technique to that ancient art of locating water. Most people will be able to do this with surprising accuracy, even with limited dowsing experience.

Lost and Found Dowsing

Common items that people dowse for are; rings, keys, wallets and items of value. Rod or pendulum dowsing can be used, the latter might be helpful at establishing which room, if any the item is in. Generally, you can use dowsing to search for any item you like. Finding it successfully will depend on where it was lost!

Missing Pets and Missing People

Police departments across the world have used dowsing to help locate missing people. Not all of them admit it, but it has been a relatively widespread practice. This is a serious use for dowsing and it can be very effective. Use a pendulum and a map; place the pendulum in a corner of the map and focus on your question; draw a line in the direction it describes and then repeat the process from another point on the map. Repeat for a third time; by this point you should have a triangle in which to focus the search. If the triangle covers a large area this can indicate that the person or animal sought is on the move, smaller triangles can suggest a specific location and you can use the pendulum within the triangle to try to establish a more detailed location. Landscape features or buildings can then be identified to search.

Directions and Safety

If you're lost, you can dowse for the best direction to take. You can also use dowsing to pick directions to avoid, when making journeys, to keep away from weather conditions or situations which may be dangerous. Don't simply rely on dowsing in this case, of course, use eyes, ears and common sense as well!

Healing and Spiritual Uses for Dowsing

Balancing the Chakras

Chakras are identified as energy points within the Aura and are associated with several ancient cultures. In recent years the art of dowsing and the Chakras have both become popular. Adherents of both traditions believe that they can be combined. Chakras are associated with different functions in the body, mind and soul and for balancing with dowsing a pendulum using a clear quartz crystal is recommended. Balancing Chakras with dowsing requires some detailed knowledge of these energy points and experience of dowsing. However, experienced dowsers often find that holding a crystal pendulum about four to six inches from each Chakra will help identify those that are out of balance. Subtle changes in the rotation, or even the sense of "friction" occurs where problems or imbalances exist.

Dowsing for Ill-health

Many dowsers have found that in addition to holding a pendulum over different areas of the body, they can diagnose problem areas by listing the major organs and components of the body. This can be done for the self or for others; lists can include organs, bones, or bodily fluids. Simply focus on each and check the pendulum's response. A simple "yes/no" question can be used as a starting point for the pendulum, with more specific questions when areas of ill-health have been identified.

Dowsing For Dosage

This is a common practice amongst many modern natural healers. Generally, it's recommended for dosage relating to herbal remedies or homeopathic remedies. This technique should be approached with extreme caution by beginners in the art of dowsing and some care even by those who are experienced. Herbs and homeopathic remedies can interact badly with other medications or cause unexpected reactions in some people. Usually, medical advice and recommendation should be sought in addition to dowsing.

Dowsing for Allergies and Intolerances (#1)

Many people suffer from the effects of mild intolerances to some food types for years, without understanding the source of the problem. Dowsing can be used to check for these, usually very effectively. Simply use a chart list of foods to discover if you, or somebody else, may have an intolerance. If so, try cutting the item in question and monitor the results. Again, a dowsing technique for the more experienced.

Dowsing for Allergies and Intolerances (#2)

Where an allergy or intolerance exists it can be important to avoid the relevant food item or ingredient. However, even modern packaging (or food in restaurants) can be misleading. Dowse to see if an ingredient is lurking in the food you are about to eat, or purchase, that you should avoid. This is often found to be a highly effective technique.

Dowsing and Auras

For those with an interest in Auras, dowsing can be an interesting way to check for strengths or weaknesses in the Aura, or areas of damage. Again, as with Chakras, some knowledge of Aura's themselves is required. Dowse either over your own or another's body to check for areas that have issues or weaknesses. Yes/no questions can also be used to check for issues with the Aura.

Psychic Wounds or Damage

Linked to Auras, understanding areas of psychic damage can also be accomplished with dowsing. Knowledge and study of the types of psychic damage is essential but dowsing is a particularly good method to use in locating or identifying this type of spiritual damage and need for healing.

Dowsing and Emotional Issues

Dowsing for buried emotions can be very effective for experienced healers. Often the cause of physical illnesses, or strongly linked to them, healers can use dowsing to identify the underlying, hidden roots of a condition. Buried emotions can be deeply buried and even the individual may not be aware of them. Pendulum dowsing can be used to rapidly identify if this is the case and healing can then begin.

Past Life Dowsing

This can be fun, even for the novice dowser, whatever your belief system. Many people from many cultures believe that we live more than one life. You can use simple "yes/no" questions to establish a connection with your past selves. This can be simply a dowsing technique used for fun or for healing techniques which focus on deeper lessons that we need to learn in this life.

General Dowsing

Many practitioners of dowsing seek information of all kinds using pendulum dowsing techniques. The following are some of the most common. However, it's important to remember that dowsing is just one way to make some of these decisions; it can be considered a very good indication of what your subconscious mind is trying to tell you! However, don't rely on dowsing to make every single decision in life; learn to follow your own common sense and feelings too!

Dowsing for Jobs

Are you unsure of which direction to take in your career or what might be a suitable career for you? Dowsing can help you to make decisions relating to jobs and the best career for you. In this case it's likely that your subconscious mind will come in to play heavily. Use a pendulum for "yes" and "no" answers or even from more specific answers. This dowsing method can be fun for anybody to try, including novices.

Locations

Use dowsing to pick places to live, visit or study. You can use a map of any scale and see which direction the pendulum suggests, or over specific neighborhoods or institutions, to get an idea of which way fate or your subconscious thinks you should travel.

Auto Questions

Use dowsing when choosing the make and model of your next car or whether to buy a specific auto. It may be possible to avoid an auto with hidden problems or find a better deal elsewhere using this method! Great if you're not an experienced mechanic!

Document Dowsing

You can use dowsing to identify problems in a document. In this case we're talking less about spell check and more about honesty or integrity of what is written. It is useful for contracts or other legal documents. Pay close attention to where the pendulum draws you in the document and think closely about any implications in the relevant section/s.

Decorating with Dowsing

Having problems deciding on a color scheme? Get that dowsing pendulum out and hover over those color charts. This can be a surprisingly effective technique even if your inner interior designer has failed you! See what the pendulum suggests and how it works when you put the elements/colors together. You might just surprise yourself.

Dowse for Energies in Your Home

Many people believe that energy points in our homes can affect our quality of life. Some locations are good and others bad. You can use dowsing very effectively to find these locations and to use them accordingly; vibrant energy spots may not be the best for your bed, for example, but great for dining tables or family rooms. Using dowsing to identify the types of energy in your home and to remove troublesome energy spots can be a great way to psychically cleanse your environment.

Feng Shui and Dowsing

This is another traditional eastern technique with similarities to dowsing for energy points. You can use dowsing to focus on the correct Feng Shui positions for beds or other items of furniture in your home. An understanding of Feng Shui is helpful for this exercise but even those with simple dowsing skills can check locations that are beneficial or otherwise.

Gardening with Rods

Not the type to support plants but to determine the best location for them in the first place. You can use dowsing to check the best locations for planting in a garden, take the plants with you and place them in different locations, where the rods indicate a "yes" is the place that those plants like best. Start digging! Dowsing with this technique is actually extremely effective (it may be another ancient use) and is a way of getting the plants themselves to give you a clue as to where they'll thrive.

Talk to the Animals

Many dowsers use the technique to hold conversations with their pets (its also been used in the past to diagnose problems with livestock). This can be a fun use for dowsing for those new to the technique. Use a chart with letters and ask any questions you like of the pet in question. Gaining a better understanding of your pet's needs can also make for a happier life for you both. Or you may simply find a great deal of satisfaction from knowing that you're already doing the best you can and your efforts are appreciated.

Interviews and Dowsing

When it comes to that dream job, you can use dowsing to identify the right clothes or jewelery for the day! This can be especially helpful if you're feeling nervous, taking the focus off the nerves and concentrating on the dowsing for a while. It can also help to give you confidence that you've created the right first impression. Some more experienced dowsers may wish to dowse to establish the sort of questions to be asked at interview, allowing you to focus your answers in the right area.

Dowsing for Relationships

You can use dowsing to establish many things about a partner, potential partner or friend. Using a chart with letters ask any question you like. Is the person honest, do they love you, is somebody deceiving you? Try to be specific with your questions and be aware that someone may be dishonest for many reasons, including to protect you from something.

Conclusion

Thank you again for reading this book!

I hope this book was able to help you to understand the facts and explode some myths behind the concept of the Third Eye and its relation to the Pineal Gland.

The next step is to try some of the steps suggested to de-calcify your Pineal Gland and begin the process of opening your own Third Eye. I hope the book will help with both and that you will soon begin to reap the full benefit of "life with three eyes"!

Finally, if you enjoyed this book, please take the time to share your thoughts and post a review on Amazon. It'd be greatly appreciated!

Thank you and good luck!

About the Author

I want to thank you for giving me the opportunity to spend some time with you!

For the last 10 years of my life I have studied, practiced and shared my love of spirituality and internal development. I kept diaries for years documenting the incredible changes that graced my life. This passion for writing has blossomed into a new chapter in my life where publishing books has become a full time career.

I feel extremely blessed and fortunate to have the opportunity to share my message with you! Each of my books are written to inspire others to explore the many aspects of their internal world. My goal is to touch the lives of others in a positive way and hopefully be the catalyst of positive change in this world

I am forever grateful for your support and I know you will get immense value through my books. I am really looking forward to serve you and give you great insight into my passions!

Your Friend

Mia Rose